SNOWSTORM OF
DOUBT
AND
GRACE

Ken & Caitriona Hume

ORIGINAL WRITING

© 2011 KEN & CAITRIONA HUME

ISBN: 978-1-908282-87-3

A CIP catalogue for this book is available from the National Library.

Published by ORIGINAL WRITING LTD., Dublin, 2011.

Printed by CLONDALKIN GROUP, Clonshaugh, Dublin 17

This book is dedicated to our beloved step-sister and step-daughter Denise, a fellow scribe who though long since passed from this life, has firmly written her story on our hearts.

To Mairead,   8/10/11

Thank you for buying this book and for your kind advice. I hope you enjoy the book

Ken Hume

Acknowledgments

Ken

First and foremost I would like to thank my mother and co-author of this book Catriona Hume or as I like to call her, mum! Without her constant support; encouragement; love; patience and belief in my ability as a poet/writer, I would never have finished this book. Sure, she wrote over a third of the pieces for the book. How much more support can you get? At times when I really doubted myself and was tempted to throw in the towel completely or felt like I had hit a creative brick wall, she was always reminding me not to forget about it; not to leave it unfinished as I had with many projects before. These words stung me and drove me on to complete Snowstorm of Doubt and Grace and get the proverbial monkey of my back.

This labour of love; this little piece of my heart, was birthed in many caffeinated conversations I had with an old friend Tony Sullivan over 2 years ago. Tony is a fellow scribe and lyricist whose prolific writing output and dedication to his craft was/is still a huge inspiration and challenge to me. He's wrote not one but 2 books of poetry and lyrics called 'Under Star And Under Sun' and 'Pilgrim In The Heartland' and you can find out more about his work and where to get it on http://www.anthonysullivan.biz/ . He helped me to believe that writing this book was actually something that I could do. And though I've not always appreciated or responded well to his advice; support and total commitment to everything he does, Snowstorm would still be just an idea in my head without him. Thank you for everything!

But when you're writing, whatever it is you're writing you need a place you can come to for ideas; for some creative stimulation, a hideout away from the rest of the world. That place for me, for the past 4 years of my life, has been a wonderful coffee bar called Chocolate Brown's situated in the middle of William Street, Tullamore, Co. Offaly. That's in Ireland for those of you not from these shores. It's hard to describe what this place or staff, past and present, means to me. Is it the 'coffee from heaven' or the happy chatter of customers? Is it the whirring of the coffee machine or the music in the background? Is it the friendliness of the staff such as Lydia; Maryna; Katerina, Eva; Ellen; Anastasia; Tanya; Imelda, Dasha and Lenka. Forgive me if there's anybody that I've forgotten or anybody's name that I may have misspelt! What about the kindness and professionalism of the shops owner's, Alan Duffy and Francoise Saliber? Or is it the cosy confines of its chocolate covered surrounds? It's all of these things and more. This is where many poems have begun; been expanded upon and indeed, completed for me. Thank you all so much for allowing me to hog the corner seats for hours on end with pen in one hand; coffee in another and notepad sitting in front of me, whilst staring dreamily into space. I'm not sure how or why you haven't thrown me out at this stage! Someday I'll be able to remove the imprint of my butt off the seat long enough to write a story about my experiences there.

Another huge influence upon me and this book has been my 9 month old niece, Aleesha Faye Hynes. She's the 'Blue Eyed Bundle of Grace' and 'Little Healer' that inspired not one, but 2 poems. Aleesha has that type of look that burns a hole right into your soul, while single-handedly helping you forget the worries you might have about life. Her insatiable curiosity; contentment and thirst for knowledge encourages me to be happy with what you have, yet always strive to know more. She has helped take my focus off me and my worries; given me renewed hope and reminded of the great capacity a baby's dependency and unconditional love has to heal and renew.

To Stella Majewsky, my former drama teacher, who once said to me that I, 'could go all the way.' Her belief in me and stubborn refusal to accept anything less than my best, gave me the confidence I needed to pursue a career in the arts. Where exactly that way leads I still do not know, but I am excited at the prospect of the journey. Thank you so much Stella, I'm sincerely indebted to you!

Lastly but by no means least, I would really like to thank Original Writing Ltd in Smithfield, Dublin without whose help; design and publishing knowhow, Snowstorm of Doubt and Grace would have remained a serious of poems and lyrics on scattered pieces of paper with pen marks through them. Garrett and Steven, I'm so grateful for all of your professionalism; patience; advice; ideas and for the final product, it looks mighty fine. Thank you so much for taking a chance on this guy and to Sr. Teresa Cahill for recommending ye to me in the first place.

Caitriona

First of all I would like to thank my husband John and all my family for their untiring belief in me. Then there's Chris and Roberto Mina, who encouraged and actively assisted in bringing previous booklets, 'You Give Me Life' and 'On Wings of Love' to print and Venus Guibone, who has been/is and always will be a motivator and inspiration. The 3 of them come all the way from the Philippines. That's not to mention the support and encouragement of very good friends Ruth, Margaret, Bonnie, Susan, Sr. Paul and Sr. Teresa.

If there's anyone that I have neglected to mention, please don't think that ye are forgotten. Take the credit that you deserve. Their support, with that of many others has helped bring my part in this book to fruition and I will be forever grateful.

Contents

Part 1
Snowstorm of Doubt

Part II
Grace

PART I
SNOWSTORM OF DOUBT

LYRICAL MIRACLE

Why do I compose each line
For my glory or to express
The purpose of a life's design
Or to mentally undress
The heart which so defines
The beauty and the mess
Of the very darkest confines
I stand ready to address

Writing and waxing lyrical
With prose ugly and sublime
I'm penning up a miracle
With all these words of mine
Little room for the intellectual
Who struggle to find the time
To comprehend the spiritual
Content of every rhyme

When I want to write
I cannot find the inspiration
It seems like one long fight
To uncover my vocation
But in the middle of the night
Words come without invitation
And helps me believe I might
Soon gain some acclamation

The Coffee Shop And Me

The coffee shop and me
Met some years ago
When I was walking by
It's portal to another world
The sweet smelling aroma
Grabbed me by the nose
And dragged me inside
To sample it's caffiene delights
And now, we're best of friends

The coffee shop and me
We meet together anytime
To conspire, to commune
In reflective caffeinated bliss
With my notepad and pen
People come and people go
We listen and observe
With outstretched senses
In this coffee shop of ideas

The coffee shop and me
We get together any day
That I am looking for
My wardrobe to poetic Narnia
Will my cup fill me with
The lyrical courage of Aslan
Or the cold; wordless touch
Of the wily White Witch
Where will this cup of coffee end?

CAUGHT IN THE CROSSFIRE

A conflict of interests, a conflict of desires
Between my faith and craft, wrapped like wires
Around this oft-divided heart
Strangling poetic thirst, spiritual hunger
And anything else it can find
On this much travelled dirt track to my soul
Littered with tainted convictions; unspoken prayers and
weary hallelujah's

Treading cautiously the minefield of split affections
Never sure whose side I'm on, but won't risk a defection
Now, for I fear that I be
Betraying heavenly devotion, creative longing
And everything else in between
This chaotic battleground called my mind
Strewn with bloodied thoughts; broken ideas and dying dreams

Standing still in the midst of chronic indecision
Get's me caught in the crossfire of someone else's vision

Painting Pictures (With Words)

Paint me a smile to end this drought
Give me something to laugh about
Instead of the sadness which has long
Invaded me, time for this song
To take a different route than the rest
You've forgiven and I've confessed
By painting pictures with words

Paint me a smile so I can start afresh
With a blank canvas so I can mesh
Past experiences and new beginnings
With the sound of angels singing
Over my new found lyrical salvation
Aided by heavenly inspiration
To paint some pictures with words

Paint me a smile with these two feet
With something melodious so I can complete
This life which you've given me
Dancing just to know that I am free
But in case I happen to trip and fall
Help me not to forget your call
To keep painting pictures with words

Paint me a smile with a paper and pen
Give me some words so I can tend
To the walking wounded and broken hearts
With ink-stained words of comfort from my cart
Of vocabulary learnt in the school of hard knocks
Time to roll up my sleeves and pull up my socks
And paint some pictures with words

Paint me a smile and I'll give them a song
Give me a tune and they can sing along
Something that will help ease their pain
And keep 'em from slowly going insane
A felonythat you will never let
A melody that won't let them forget
Those pictures I painted with words

Silver Screen Of Memory

My reality is a world of dreams
Some broken; some unfulfilled
Played to me on that silver screen
Of memory that's not yet stilled

There hope and regret perform for free
In my head and for my heart
One promises great things to be
The other mourns what must depart

Dreams of plans yet to be
Reflections of love gone by
Join in uneasy matrimony
Behind the floodgates of my eye

Trodding the tearducts of sorrow
With footsteps from the past
They dance slowly to the blow
Of the lonely trumpet blast

That plays frequently in my head
With the beat of my own drum
And tells me my dreams aren't dead
Until my time on earth has run

That Awkward Boy

You wonder why sometimes, I don't know what to say
You wonder why sometimes, I won't come out and play
Nice with all the other kids, who seem to know their way

Bridge
But that awkward boy insists on following me
Shadowing everywhere I go; shaping everything I see, and...

Chorus
I still see that awkward boy, masquerading as a man
That same awkward, nervous boy who continues to stand
On the outskirts of life and love, reaching out his hand
Looking for somebody to give this awkward boy a chance

You wonder why sometimes, I always go astray
You wonder why sometimes, I always act this way
But it's never been my intention to push people away

Bridge
It's that awkward boy...

Chorus
I still meet that awkward, masquerading as a man
That same awkward, nervous boy who continues to stand
On the outskirts of life and love, reaching out his hand
Looking for somebody to give this awkward boy a chance

Bridge

It's that awkward boy who insists on following me
Shadowing everywhere I go and everyone I see, and...

Chorus

I still see that awkward boy masquerading as a man
That same awkward, nervous boy who continues to stand
On the outskirts of life and love, reaching out his hand
Looking for somebody to give this awkward boy a chance

Tripping Over Myself

I won't drown my sorrows in glasses of wine
Bottles of whiskey or coronas and lime
That numbs my senses and slows down my mind
Leaves me struggling to uncover some rhymes
Crying out with some prayers for divine

Chorus
Intervention, it's not my intention
To keep on falling; tripping over myself
Reinvention, I need your direction
So, I'll keep calling on you for your help

Won't be a slave anymore to this widescreen T.V
That has 1,000 channels on with nothing to see
Mobile phones; I-Pod's and web technology
Lure me with promises of false security
That slowly detach me from life's reality

Chorus
Intervention,...

Won't look back over mistakes that I've made
Love that I've lost, thought's I've replayed
In my mind, or silly games that I've played
With time, isn't it time I stayed
In one place long enough and prayed... for

Chorus (x2)
Intervention,...

Sleeping Heart
(Does It Still Beat?)

I'm looking at this girl walk by
Through the coffee shop window pane
Oh, my heart stirs and I wonder why
I've been so long out of the game
Of love, that once made me try
Flush those feelings down the drain
But it's impossible to deny
Her beauty is greater than my pain
Do I go...

Chorus
Fishing for just one more chance
In that still sea of tired romance
To see if my sleeping heart still beats
Does my sleeping heart still beat?
Hoping that I can cross that line
Be more than a one day Valentine
And see if my sleeping heart still beats
Will it beat because of her?

The next day she stops walking
Smells the coffee ad comes inside
I try hard but I can't stop gawking
At her, as she orders, then sits beside
Me and starts gently talking
To me, but my tongue gets tied

I feel that old fear is stalking
My mind and leaving me paralysed

Chorus
Fishing for just one more...

Time for this caterpillar heart of mine
To crawl out of its cocoon
But I'm too scared of love's sunshine
I'd rather it let me stew in
The comforting loneliness one more time
Easier than flying to the moon
Or Venus if I could read the signs
On these butterfly wings, I assume
It'd be easier to let down a line
And go...

Chorus (X2)
Fishing for just one more chance
In that still sea of tired romance
To see if my sleeping heart still beats
Does my sleeping heart still beat?
Hoping that I can cross that line
To be more than a one day Valentine
And see if my sleeping heart still beats
Will it beat because of her?

Tough Cookie With A Tender Heart

She's a tough cookie with a tender heart
Playing love with a rookie in a bit part
In the movie of her life
That needs a fresh romance
But she's been burnt before
And is scared to take a chance

On this kind but inexperienced man
With a lot of love but without a plan
For the lady's tender heart
That needs a little consoling
But this man might ride away
When the credits start a rolling

On this tragic tale of amorous attrition
In a hopeless romantic on constant audition
For the role of damsel in distress
That needs someone to save the day
But she's tired of playing that part
Now she needs someone who'll stay

364 Other Days

'Valentine's is but one day a year'
When roses, chocolates and teddy bears rear
Their mocking, greedy heads and sneer
At the lovesick and lonely who rightly fear

The stigma of the singleton on this day
When adults, adolescents and little ones all play
Their needy, dating rituals and say
I love you, don't leave me and stay

With me forever in Cupid's maze
But they forget about the 364 other day's
There with the 364 other way's
To show how much you care and raise

The level of your love and devotion
That's not just about the roses and emotion
Or brought about by some magic potion
It takes some hard work swimming through the ocean

Of commitment with a lot of self-sacrifice,
Patience; strength and consideration to be concise
It's not always brought about being nice
But by knowing when to step up and fight

For her or him
On the 364 other days
In the 364 other way's
And not just Valentine's

YES, I CAN SEE YOUR HEARTBREAK

Yes, I can see your heartbreak
As you mourn your love's demise
It's etched all over your worn face
And written in your eyes

Yes, I can see your heart break
Through the bathroom door
As the teardrops force the ache
Through the skin, onto the floor

Yes, I can feel your heart break
Every time I take your hand
When we embrace, your body shakes
And I try to understand

But, I can't know your heartbreak
Because I have never been
Where you have been or had to take
In what your eyes have seen

On The Outside (She Might Seem)

Part I
On the outside, she seems so tough
But inside, she's made of softer stuff
Than you might realise.

Because she's really had enough
Of having a life; so hard, so rough
And she has grown wise,

To those promises made off the cuff
By men who think they've got the stuff
That all ends up in lies.

Part II
She might seem angry from the start
It's just a mask for her great big heart
That has a lot to give.

So, if you're willing and your smart
You'll quickly figure out your part
In her life and forgive,

Her when her emotions start to fly
And she raises her hands to the sky
She got no alternative.

Woman With A Million Thoughts

A woman with a million thoughts
Running around her mind
Each vying for a place she's sought
For years to find
A place that makes sense to her
Peaceful like the vast sea
To get lost in the realms of nature
A place where she can just be

Song For A Girl

Small girl, big heart
Really don't know where to start
Pretty girl, happy vibe
Is how I would describe
A woman destined to be
A young girl for eternity

Chorus
This is a song for a girl
Just to say, I think you're swell
Thank you for the joy you give
With this vibrant life you live

Dark hair, big smile
She stops to talk a little while
Sing a song, dance a lot
A fragile girl is what she's not
For her strength lies inside
With a bliss you cannot hide

Chorus
This is a song...

Peter Pan, Thumbelina
You move like a ballerina
Quick to laugh, slow to age
You could grace any page
Of a glossy magazine
Looking like a beauty Queen

Chorus (x2)
This is a song...

You Draw The Truth From Me

I'm dealing with some things that I'd never dealt
Feeling things that I never thought could be felt
Peeling away layers from the past and the welt
From your verbal assault that's all beginning to melt
My heart and,

You draw the truth from me, like a knife draws blood
It hurts at first cut baby, but soon it's pouring out like a flood
Of crimson covered; pent-up hurts, as you pull down the hood
Of disguise from over my eyes, exposing what I thought could
Not be exposed;

Now, I'm taking a look at myself to see what's gone wrong
With the opportunities I've had and why they are gone
While tearing down the walls I've built up for too long
By offering the same excuses and singing the same old song
See how,

You draw the truth from me, like a knife draws blood
It hurts at first cut baby, but soon it's pouring out like a flood
Of crimson covered; pent-up hurts, as you pull down the hood
Of disguise from over my eyes, exposing what I thought could
Not be exposed;

If I did easy babe, then I wouldn't be with you

If I did easy babe, then I wouldn't be with you
Don't have to please me babe, just have to look into
My eyes, they'll tell you no lies because they be feeling a bit blue
Not just a colour for me but speaking for my mood

When we fall out or fall in
To a rut, yet I've never been
More alive and excited about what lies ahead
You've revived & invited my soul in from the dead

REMEMBER WHEN
(MORE THAN JUST FRIENDS)

Remember when we talked along the path late one night?
You asked me if I'd walk you home while under the street light
'Yes', I said, 'Of course I would'. And you smiled so bright
And yet so vulnerable, made me want to hold you so tight, so

Chorus
Tight in my heart is where I hold you
Because my arms just can't reach that far
Tight in my arms is where I'll keep you
Because even though time has gone too far
I remember when, yes I remember when
We could have been... more than just friends

Remember when we got to your door, at the end of dream street?
You asked me if I'd like to come in; take off my coat and have a seat
'There's nothing more I'd like to do', I said,
'But I just can't move my feet'
So we stood instead on fates doorstep, and embraced
as you began to weep... and

Chorus
Tight in my heart...

Remember when I just held you in my shaking arms as you cried
And told me about the guy who left you behind, how undignified
Of him to leave you this way, couldn't have done that if I tried
Then you said, 'I think you're really handsome',
well I could have died
So,

Chorus
Tight in my heart...

Remember when you kissed me then,
right out of the night's deep blue
Didn't take my favourite colour could make my dreams come true
But before we could begin, you told me that we were through
Could never be 'more than just friends',
you broke my heart in two
But,

Chorus (x2)
Tight in my heart...

Don't Know Why

Don't know why I ever said it
Don't know why I let you go
Must've been a rush of blood to the head
Now our goodbye is embedded
In little capsules of tears that flow

Through the recesses of my mind
As I dare not let them be spoken
And shatter my world with the reality
That a little part of me has been broken

Don't know why I ever said it
Don't know why I let you go
I lost the plot and broke your heart
Now our goodbye is embedded
In little capsules of tears that flow

Through the arteries of my heart
As I dare not let them come outside
And stain my cheeks with evidence
That a little part of me has died

Don't know why I ever said it
Don't know why I let you go
You're the best thing that ever happened
Now our goodbye is embedded
In little capsules of tears that flow

Through the blood in my veins
As I dare not let them burst through
And puncture my skin like you punctured my heart
Now every part of me wants to be with you

Hangin' On A Broken Wing

Saying goodbye is the hardest thing
When it pierces you to the very core
Letting go doesn't really bring
The release you've been hoping for
Maybe If I find a new song to sing
It'll help bandage up the sores
That's left me hangin on a broken wing
And a prayer, to keep me off the floor

Of despair and brokenness
Tell me where is the joke in this?
Should be in the air with you no less
Not hangin' on a broken wing,
I confess…

There's day's when I've wanted to ring
You a million times and say
Sorry, sorry for the fool I've been
And letting you slip away

SUMMER SOUL

You bring me joy with every day
Despite the doubt which haunts my way
You make it easy for me to see
That you're the best thing in life for me
You make me laugh when I want to cry
And give me wings so that I can fly
You wipe away those silent tears
And release me from those nagging fears

Chorus
With you the sun always shines
In my clouds, you are my silver line
You're light filled that empty hole
When you became my Summer Soul

Every time you walk into the room
My darkness, your light does consume
A surge of life runs through my being
I still can't believe what I'm seeing
You make me laugh, but you're no clown
And turned my world right upside down
When I'm with you, I feel complete
I feel like dancing to you beat

Chorus
With you the sun...

When I look upon your face
I see a reflection of His grace
A blinding light surges from within
That purges me from lingering sin
I was lost, but now am found

When you picked me up off the ground
You shone your light all over me
Paid my debt and set me free

Chorus
With you the sun always shines
In my clouds, you are that silver line
Your light filled that empty hole
When you became my Summer Soul

Sounds Of Summer

Seems like the sun has come out today
From it's hiding place behind the grey
Shining on the kids as they play
In the swimming pool or on the streets
Or sitting on the park bench seats
Laughing loudly as they meet
Friends they haven't seen in awhile
Go to place they haven't been, all while
The car roof's down for another mile

Chorus
I want to hear the sounds of summer
To feel the warmth of it's pure rays
Taking me back when I was younger
And caught up in a sun-soaked gaze

But nobody knows how long it will stay
With us, before it ups and goes away
Sun please let us know, so we can lay
Down on this soft grass and feel your heart
Once more and walk upon our bare feet
Whilst basking in those booming beats
From the radio, turn up that dial
Open that window and let down a smile
As you take in that sizzling summer style

Chorus
I want to hear the sounds of summer
To feel the warmth of its pure rays
Taking me back when I was younger
And caught up in a sun-soaked gaze

Sunglasses Of Disguise

Hiding my cornea's from the sunlight in the skies
Hiding the strain from the prying world's eyes
Hiding is something that these sunglasses of disguise
Help me do so well,
But they can't hide me from the why's
No they can't hide me from the why's

Hiding the dark bags from the early morning sunrise
Hiding the swelling from the prying world's eyes
Hiding is something that these sunglasses of disguise
Help me do so well,
But they can't hide me from the lies,
No they can't hide me from the lies

BLUE EYED BUNDLE OF GRACE

Aleesha Faye, you caught us a little by surprise
When you launched your premature escape
From your amniotic cocoon to coo's and sigh's
And entranced eyes, as your mother gaped
At the sight of you, exhausted and overjoyed
Whimpering; helpless and bare
Handed to your father, one of those celluloid
Moments. Timeless. Precious. Rare.

Aleesha Faye, our lives will never be the same
Now that you're here with us
Sleepless days; midnight feeds and nappy changes
But we think you're worth the fuss
Because you give us so much joy by simply being
In the same room and breathing in
The same air, smiling; stretching and even seeing
With squinted eyes, makes life worth believing

Aleesha Faye, it's nice to meet you, my niece
You maybe newborn to this world
But you've already stolen a little piece
Of my heart, when you curled
Into my arms, laying there happily asleep
Arm raised over your face
Shuffling and smiling in a dream so deep
A blue-eyed bundle of grace

Unemployment Town
(Tumbleweed of Promise)

Outside, I hear the distant thudding of some hooves
Reverberating loudly through this dusty ground
I kinda get the feeling I'll be the next guy to move
Out of prosperity place into unemployment town

Chorus
Unemployment town
It's bigger than it used to be
No optimism to be found
Here, in this jobless valley
So barren and desolate
Hopeless and desperate
Is this unemployment town

Well, he rode in on his dark horse of gloom
To a town filled with recession and empty chairs
To bury my dying business in this desert tomb
And pierce my skin with a jobless bullet of despair

Chorus
Unemployment town...

Now that this heartless cowboy has come to me
And is knocking impatiently on my front door
Outside, his black horse is neighing indignantly
In the mangled face of that lonely tiger's roar

Chorus
Unemployment town...

Closing
Then I see a tumbleweed of promise
Blow through this job-forsaken town
On his white steed of love and grace
To sweep your feet up off the ground
He's the lone rider of our salvation
Sheriff of the lost and found
With a water skin full of hope
To quench your thirst
In this unemployment town

Hurried Ignorance

You always walk right by
Where I sit down on the street
Never bothering to try
My special needs to meet
You have so much to give
But you only want to take
Your chosen way to live
Is by how much you make

Chorus
I'm humiliated and in a mess
There's nothing I can do
To make your ignorance hurt me less
And help me get through
Another day of hopelessness
Without begging you

I always see you in a rush
Looking for an education
In the constant shove and push
To find you destination
You say you're in a hurry
"I'll get you next time"
The world demands you scurry
To stop would be a crime

Chorus
I'm humiliated and...
When you've finally found
What you're looking for
I might not be around

To say I told you so
But, if you'd stop a while
And spend a moment with me
You'd see beyond my broken smile
Into a heart of misery

Chorus (x2)
I'm humilated and...

Around The Bend

Well, hello there old friend
It sure has been a while
Since I saw you around the bend
With a bottle of empty smiles
That promised it would mend
Your many trials
But, it only seems to send
You further into denial...

Chorus
Of drunken memories; hazy memories
Of who you used to be
Sunken memories in raging seas
Of dreams you'll never see

So, I'll see you soon old friend
As I must be getting on
Before you reel me in again
With some lies and then we're gone
Because when I have to lend
You money, it won't be long
Untill we're staggering around that bend
Singing the same old songs

Chorus
Of drunken memories...

Now, I say goodbye old friend
I must finish this sad rhyme
You stayed drinking to the end
And died while in your prime
Is there anybody who can tend
This broken heart of mine
While I carry you around this bend
Shoulder-high for one last time

Chorus (x2)

Clay Of Mortality

Didn't feel the grief till just the other day
Though, I thought I had been dealing with the pain
But now I'm covered with cold blankets of grey
Thoughts of my departed dad lying in the clay...
The clay of mortality

Didn't know that I could ever feel this way again
Like I'm a child that needs soothing from the pain
But, my father isn't around to give me shelter from the rain
Instead, he's lying still in 8 feet of clay...
The clay of mortality

Now, I'm not so sure if I can bring myself to play
With my own kids when my daddy has gone away
I don't know what to do with them or even what to say
So, I let them run around while I think about the clay...
The clay of mortality

One thing I do know is that I'll have to take each day
At a time; for a time, because that's the only way
I can cope with this loss, so I look up to heaven and sway
With prayerful groanings and tears falling on the clay
The clay of mortality

Still Live On There

It's been so long
Since you went up and gone
Your way outta here
But there was no fear
In those fading eyes
Not even surprise
Because you always knew
Where you were going, so

Chorus
There in heaven is where you'll be
You'll be there for eternity
Least, that's what you always said to me
And someday, that's where I'll be...

That was some time ago
The truth is I still miss you so
My loss is heaven's gain
Does nothing much to ease my pain
Keeps me awake at night
Prayin' for that kinda light
You always talked about
When you were here, but

Chorus
There in heaven...

Sometimes I'd like to see
You standing there in front of me
Tellin' me I need direction
Not just a reflection
Of you in my dreams
Which are never as they seem
Feels like you never left
For you still live on there

Chorus (x2)
There in heaven...

It's Okay To Say No Sometimes

It's okay to say no sometimes
When you're tired and had a long day

It's okay to say no sometimes
And look for another way

It's okay to say no sometimes
Even though your kids will ask you why?

And it's okay to say no sometimes
When your friends are getting high

It's okay to say no sometimes
To that guy who's selling pills

It's okay to say no sometimes
Though it'd help you pay the bills

It's okay to say no sometimes
When they offer you a drink

It's okay to say no sometimes
When you need some time to think

It's okay to say no sometimes
To protect their innocence

It's okay to say no sometimes
When you're short on confidence

It's okay to say no sometimes
When there's no-one there to advise

It's okay to say no sometimes
When you're principles won't compromise

It's okay to say no sometimes
In a world that always says yes
To go against the flow sometimes
Is hard but earns you respect
Of some... this time
It's okay to say no!

WORDLESS CONVERSATIONS

Wordless conversations on a barstool seat
Between two men who've never met before
Sharing an unspoken bond in this ferment retreat

Wordless conversations on a canal-bank line
Between an ageing father and his son
Fishing for the perfect words, pulling on borrowed time

Wordless conversations on a crumpled marraige bed
Between a jaded husband and wife
Mourning silently for a love that's long been dead

A Million Other Things
(Everything But Right)

You can say it's poor memory
You may call it an oversight
You may call it a million other things
Still, it's everything but right

You can call it your only option
You can say that there is no light
You can call it a million other things
Still, it's everything but right

You can say it's a half-truth
You can call it little and white
You can call it a million other things
Still, it's everything but right

You can call it convenient
You may say that things are tight
You can call it a million other things
Still, it's everything but right

You can call it feeling lonely
You may say it was for just one night
You can call it a million other things
Still, it's everything but right

Make The Bad News Go Away

Another bomb goes off, another baby dies
Another building crashes down and we look up to the skies
Another son goes off to war while another mother cries
At another son who takes his life and we all wonder why

Chorus
Why does this keep happening?
Why does nothing seem to change?
Oh, the shape of this world we're in
Make the bad news go away
Please, make the bad news go away

Another child's innocence is forever stolen
By another man of the cloth while another head is rollin'
When another job is lost & another family need consolin'
For another car crash fatality, how have we fallin'?!

Chorus
Why does this keep...

Another promise broken, another family falls apart
Another institution crumbles by deceitfulness of the heart
Another love unspoken, leaves another woman to depart
To another man, in another home, where did it all start?

Chorus
Another earthquake brings another country to it's knees
While another house is flooded in water and desperate plea's
For another government with more heart; hope and honesty
Before another man falls into debt or business into bankruptcy

Chorus
Why does this keep happening?
Why does nothing seem to change?
Oh, the shape of the world we're in
Make the bad news go away
Please, make the bad news go away

Stop Trying So Hard

Stop trying so hard my son
You weren't made to walk this path alone
Stop thinking you're the only one
Who knows what it's like, pick up the phone
Call a friend and let them know
What's going on before you go
Stumbling over hurdles you didn't see
Because you were trying so hard to be
All strong and self-sufficient

Stop carrying that load my son
You weren't made to hold this weight alone
Stop thinking you're the only one
Who knows what it's like, pick up the phone
Call a friend and let them know
What's going on before you go
Falling under the weight of it all
The weight of the world
You have on your shoulders

Stop fighting the world my son
You weren't made to throw those punches alone
Stop thinking you're the only one
Who's been beaten down, pick up the phone
Call a friend and let them know
What's going on before you go
Walking right into that knockout punch
Because you acted on a hunch
That someone else was against you

Worship And Regret

A fellowship sweet, a fellowship divine
A place where I used to come, to seek and find
Something deeper, more intimate
A place where I can weep or investigate

Things that are wrong, mistakes that I've made
In your presence long, I cannot evade
The reality of my weakness burns a hole inside
My soul, but meekness is no excuse to hide!

I want to worship you in Spirit and in Truth
But I'm haunted by the errors of my youth
Fearful of the mess that's buried in my heart
Let your holiness come and tear it all apart

Knowing that I can't just turn back the years
Fills me with some sadness and a well of tears
But, you dry my eyes with a joyous melody
Words which are wise and a love that is free

So I want to thank you for all that you've done
Lord, the times you've pulled me up when I came undone
In a fog of lonely dissatisfaction and despair
Mental interrogations soothe by a little prayer

STILL
(SHADOWS IN THE SUN)

Still seeing those same things, in those same dreams
 I wish I hadn't a done
Those things that scar your memory and make you want to run
Far away from anywhere that reminds you of anyone
That hurt you and forever cast some
Shadows on your sun
Some shadows on your sun

Still walking those dole queue's in those old shoes
that you gave me last spring
Alas, none of that fortune you hoped that it would bring
Has come my way, and now I'm shuffling slowly to the brink
Of jobless oblivion, in this Post Office full of
Those shadows in the sun
Hopeless shadows in the sun

Still clinging to that same faith that helps console &
contemplate this world in which I live
That type of faith that stirs my soul and offers me an alternative
To this forever changing earth pouring through the sieve
Of eternity, where uncertainty colours the sky
With more shadows in the sun
More shadows in the sun

Still fighting back those same old doubts that raise a
familiar shout whenever I'm about to fly
The type of doubt that consumes your mind and gives
you a million reasons why
Not to take that job, ask out that girl or dare to even try
Follow that daydream all the way
Through those shadows in the sun
Those shadows in the sun

Still seeing,
still walking,
still running,
still clinging,
still praying,
still fighting
still dreaming...
STILL!

DEVIL'S DOUBT HALLELUJAH

Another sleepy Sunday morning creeps through the window pane
In blinding layers of heaven's light that pierce my groggy brain
It pulls me from the land of dreams where I always call
upon your name
On my knees, scarred a little by the secret sting of shame

Another bang of the drum reverberates through the years
Triggering happy memories of soul songs and conquered fears
But the cold grey shadow of devil's doubt still rears
It's ugly head and whispers "you're nothing" in my ears

Another strum of the guitar starts cutting through the lies
But can barely be heard above the many questions and heavy sighs
Of some struggling believers so confused they cry
Silently, in veiled worship, dreaming of bluer skies

But, I'll sing another hallelujah amidst the throng of weary saints
Yearing for that youthful fire that's grown a little faint
And the blood red colour of God's grace to repaint
That faded yawning canvas of a dying faith

When I Look Upon Your Face

When I look upon your face
And see the beauty of your grace
It amazes me that you see
The deepest, darkest parts of me
Yet your love is unconditional
For someone so unexceptional

When I look upon your face
I remember all you've erased
Helping me through my sin
My heart can scarcely take it in
That you forget when you forgive
Makes it easy for me to live

When I look upon your face
I consider when you took my case
With all the odds stacked against
You came and stood in my defense
Paid the price to set me free
From an uncertain eternity

Now I look upon your face
Happily a part of the human race
No longer content to be
Hidden away in my own reality
I'm grateful that You are my friend
And will be so to the very end

Sentimental Over A Fool

"Fool; fool", you'd always say
But you were no fool to us
Like a broken record, you'd play
But I always thought you had it sussed
Mister, what made you this way?
A little strange yet humorous
Mister, you always made our day
When came in to visit us

"I just died", was your refrain
To anyone you'd meet
Some thought you were insane
Others a sad form of sweet
Mister, were you in pain?
And no else could see it.
Mister, will we see you again
Shuffling down our streets?

"Buzz off", you would blurt out
To anyone who passed by
Not sure what you were on about
More so, the reason why
Across the street, would come the shout
"Hey mister, buzz off", you'd sigh
Place the burning cigarette in your mouth
And say, "I'm off, goodbye!"

Rollercoaster Mind

Writing just to find a way
To make sense of the thougths that sway
Around my rollercoaster mind
Fighting against the prey
Of doubt that just eats away
And keeps me on rewind

Writing while all the kids play
Games on one more sunny day
But my rollercoaster mind
Keeps me on the fence today
Wondering just what to say
And I get left behind

Writing while I'm feeling down
Helps me cope with life's merry go round
And I begin to rewind
Keeps me fighting off the sound
Of my voice that rebounds
Off my rollercoaster mind

Unforgiving Sun
(Dark Eyes Squint for Mercy)

It's a sunny, Sunday afternoon
Inebriated bones are slowly stirring
As we slowly emerge from our cocoon.
And the coffee machine begins whirring
Like our heads, the heat makes us swoon

As we gingerly make our way outside
The fierce morning sun unforgiving
Of last night's escapades, as our dark eyes
Squint for mercy, and we're driven
For the only place where we can hide

And converse about whatever dumb
Things we may have done, but can't remember
Think it all went downhill after the rum
Like that crazy night back in mid-September
But all vices look brighter under the sun

It's okay though, we always have Facebook
To see if we were caught on camera, tagged
In some state of compromising debauchery, look
There we are, our pristine reputations dragged,
Through the mud of intoxication, think we're stuck

PART II
GRACE

SNOWSTORM OF GRACE

I love the two beautiful cherry blossom trees in my garden. For about two weeks every year, they are profusely overhung with millions of pink blossoms, which are a joy to behold. Sadly, their life-span is brief. The first windy day in April heralds their punctuated demise. Looking out my window, I see this snowstorm or whirlwind of fluffy pink petals in flight from their branches. The wind swirls them about in mid-air, before coming to earth in my immediate neighbourhood. Before touching the ground, they perform a spiral dance for me and then come to rest, creating a perfect floral carpet. The pleasure was brief – but what a performance!

SPECIAL DELIVERY

Welcome, welcome little one, surprising us all with your
own early arrival into this strange new world,
planned for you from time immemorial.
Skin on skin, body on body, warmth on touch
Loving this awesome little human being,
who trusts beyond our understanding
Punching the air with strong little limbs
Reaching out eagerly into the unknown
Touching base with unfamiliar faces who need to find
their inner child.
Sleeping the sleep of the innocent, allowing angelic smiles
to surprise and enthral us.
What dreams you dream, of whence you came,
are yours alone.
O beautiful child, you have already touched lives and hearts;
there is a quiet purpose to your presence among us, little healer.
Those deep blue pools for eyes seeping into our very beings
on a journey of discovery
Snuggle into our lives where hope springs eternal and
stir the embers of love.

WE DON'T GET IT!
(DEDICATED TO MARY D)

After all this time we don't get it, do we? What we don't get is, that love is all that matters. What the world offers, will never surpass or even come close to what real love means.

The love of family; the love of God; deeds done for each other out of love, not grudgingly or selfishly; reaching out to those impoverished in spirit, and reflecting the love of God; acknowledging that we are who we are, because of the greatest act of love this world has ever known, that one Man would give up his life for us on a cross.

We seldom hear that message any more in this merry-go-round world, where we rarely take time to get off and reflect why we are here and to where we are ultimately bound.

There are people we meet every day who radiate love by being who they are and by just being alive. They see beyond the obvious, the mundane; they have a vision of how things might be or should be, and pray, that someday, someone will listen, will take their time to hear their hearts cry.

These people are human first of all; they get frustrated with being blocked at every turn; being ignored and sidelined. But they have a spirit that is driven, not by the world, but by God who gives the grace to rise above all of these obstacles and reach out to the walking wounded among us. They leave their mark in a love that can never be erased

May we take up their mantle and go out into the world with their message of love when we get it!

Doonloughan Beach

Deserted today, but for one parked car and one middle-aged lady slowly sauntering along the sandy beach in County Galway, turning her head now and then as if to recapture once more, where the wind came from.

The wind blows my hair, whipping it's strands every which way, uncontrollable and unmanageable. I make my way through the golden sandy shingle, like a child again, cupping handfuls of tiny coloured stone, allowing the sand ripple through my fingers, in awe at the extent of this beautiful spectacle. What is it about a golden beach that brings about this sense of wonder in us?

The sand is soft underfoot and cushions each footstep, as I meander between rocks covered with seaweed deposited by the tide. The tide is well out now, but I am conscious of the need to be alert, and not lose my sense of time in this peaceful haven.

I have always sought out unusual coloured stones at the beach, and here is no exception, as shades green; rust; turquoise and marble effect of black and white attracts my attention. I cannot take it all with me, but select as many as I can carry, to take home for some decorative purpose, at a later time.

So many pleasant distractions and so much more still to see!

Reaching green hillocks, adorned with vivid purple and yellow flowers, I stand a while and become aware of how close I am to the Atlantic, as I look out from this coastline.

This is spine-tingling stuff, and I know I am in a very special place!

I negotiate safe stepping stones, as my curiosity leads me to explore behind high rocks, where I discover rock pools and sheltered sandy dunes; ideal hideaways I thought, if one needed a quite retreat from passing day trippers.

Totally unfazed by human distraction, one lone seagull explores through a mound of seaweed on the beach, with her beak, tossing it about from side to side as she seeks her next nibble probably.

No competition here!

Making my way back on a path parallel to the one I had taken earlier, I noticed the sky darken ahead.

Carrying a bag with a motley collection of stones chosen earlier, I was conscious of the peace of the place, and very reluctant to leave it behind. There was no sun overheard that day, so a walk on the beach would not have been the main attraction for most people

Fortunately for me, I came to this place on the recommendation of a friend, made a connection with one of nature's beautiful gifts; freely given, freely received.

Quietly and gently, it has healed; cleansed and renewed my Spirt!

Autumnal Bliss

Watching the brown and golden autumn leaves dance pirouette like across the tarmac and along the pathways, carried by the sudden spurt of wind, onwards and upwards. Often leaves lying flat on the ground as if attached leech like, immobile, unstirred by the other activity, create a speckled carpet to adorn the greyness.

Remembering walking along tree-lined country lanes, thickly blanketed with beautiful shades of brown, golden russet leaves; shuffling feet through the thick pile and hearing the rustling noises timidly interrupting the peaceful countryside. It was another world away from the active hive of town and city life where contrasting sounds polluted the air. If one was fortunate enough to pick blackberries along the way, there was the bonus of succulent homemade jam in the months ahead.

The smells carried by the wind were at once perfumed and farmyard, reflecting the life and times of the inhabitants scattered across the fields and lanes with its ebb and flow of daily activity.

It is so easy to empty the mind and renew the body and spirit here, where burdens are lifted and float away beyond the realm of awareness.

A calm, peaceful energy overtakes and envelops, immersing one in total serenity, lingering long after the experience.

I'm In A Time Warp Of Autumnal Bliss!

What Am I Doing?

Writing words on empty pages
Filling spaces with print of little meaning

Where do they come from?
Where do they need to be expressed?

Do they need to be read by someone
who thinks they understand their source?

Or do I need to get them past the
caverns of my mind before even
I can fathom their depths?

Why do I write this language that
finds expression in this way
and raises more questions than
answers?

Have I left a space which gives
birth to more unanswerable questions?

I can but wait for sweet clarity!

THE COFFEE – BEAN COMPANY

We are in coffee – bean country
In the heart of creative company
Where words flow easily to communicate, obliterate,
Reverberate where they will
We dissect, inject, connect and adjudicate
On literary and poetic events
We formulate, disseminate, eliminate from our
Poetic prowess all unwordy creations
In the throes of dissertations we are elated
Exalted and elevated to higher plains
What matter the illusions, intrusions and infusions
From would – be pedants
We continue to proliferate, pontificate and
Pronounce on matters central to your theme
We lift up your dreams, bursting at the seams
For expression and education
The world needs to know that we exist
In our creative coffee–bean company
We will give voice to the inner expressions
Of our being with or without you
We have something to say, we have designs
On your mind, we pen it today

HIDE ME

Hide me behind the laurels of this world
Out of sight of would-be-plaudits
Keep me out of view, save that of knowing my own light

Where is there to hide in a world
That seeks to see itself in its own glory
With little knowledge of whence it came?

Can you find a place for me
Which seeks not to magnify its own greatness
But knows its place among the stars?

It's there amid the dross of egoism
A treasure hidden in a world where self's alive
A humble jewel in a world where soul has died

WHISPERING

Whispering in the corridor, whispering in the street
Whispering in the alleyway, where the secrets meet
Whispering in the coffee-bar, whispering in the mall
Whispering on the telephone, with that private call
Whispering about your neighbour, whispering about your friend
Whispering about your workmate, is this the common trend?

Another good name taken, another life dragged down
Another whispered secret distorted truth once known
The confidence then promised, the lips that then were sealed
Now open at the slightest whim where nothing is concealed

To whisper is to softly speak; to breathe a word; to sigh
To speak conspiratorially or confidence deny
It can also be a rumour; an undertone; a hiss
A suggestion inappropriate where truth can go amiss
If anything here written has touched a chord within
Then only you can deal with it and start anew again

SIDE BY SIDE

Side by side I journey, on the long road home
I do not travel solo, I do not go alone
If I think the walk is only mine, how foolish I can be
It takes another step with mine to help me truly see

Side by side we journey, just one step at a time
We cannot look too far ahead or many mountains climb
Just day by day we travel, and hour by hour we take
Letting each moment happen, letting our senses wake

Side by side we travel, along life's bumpy road
It's not easy on our own, carrying a heavy load
Let us share it out among us, there is no need for pride
When our burden's lightened, our heart-strings are untied

If we just walk together, knowing how we've tried
Remembering our experiences, remembering times we've cried
We may never mind the loneliness, never feel the pain
Because we know the journey, has not always been in vain

THOUGHTS

What happens when the soul divides and spirits cannot blend?
The mind is full of ups and downs, no happy in-betweens
It draws you up, it pulls you down, it casts you back and forth
You are overwhelmed, you are down and out,
you cannot stand the force

You try to tranquilize the ups, and stimulate the downs
And maybe find the pathway that is not too out of bounds
The wave of sadness overcomes and helps to give release
To all the pent up thoughts of doom that are crying out for peace

These thoughts can carry us on wings to far off dreamy places
Or keep us in the state of things where nothing ever changes
The sun can always shine in us and make our faces glow
Or clouds can come and spoil the view and bring our spirit low
We have the gift within ourselves to feed that wayward spirit
To bring our soul to life in us and see each other's merit

HIDDEN LIFE

Tiny boxes stuck together, rising to the sky
To right and left, above, below, nowhere left to fly
There is no room to move around, to grow up or to hide
But life is here for young and old, where freedom is denied
The symbols of a life ill-spent are painted on the walls
The sounds of living echoing the conflict in their souls

How can they see the sunshine, how can they touch the grass?
How can they smell the flowers, do they just let it pass?
Do you think the spirit dies here; did it ever have a life?
Or just a mere existence amidst poverty and strife

When the curse of calm indifference casts a pall upon this place
You can see how it's reflected in the look on every face
There is a place for everyone beneath the skies above
But here above all others, there's a need for hope and love

Soulless Vacuum

Dehumanized misfits
Criminals
Delinquents
Victims of divorce
Defensive and lonely enemies of mankind

Where do they belong?
Where are their families?
Where are their homes?
Do we live in a society whose capacity for love has died?

Abandoned children
Disappearing in a vacuum
The ground shifting under their feet
No solid foundation, no trust
Enter disillusionment, fear, betrayal

Twisted minds and hearts
Crippled for ever
Dispirited, lost souls
On the brink of despair
Do we say, "Thank God I am not like the rest of men?"

WHERE WILL YOU SLEEP?

Where will you sleep tonight, my friend?
Where will you lay your head?
On a four-poster bed in a grand hotel
Or a cold wooden couch in a prison cell
Maybe a shop front or an empty shed
With a bottle or two for company, or a mind doped into eternity
In a dull; dreary ward with a tranquilized mind,
your lonely vigil keep

Where will you lay your head tonight?
When the stars in the sky are shining bright?
In an abandoned car or under a bridge
Covered with blankets or overhung ledge
Immune to the cold or the frost and the snow
With no hope in sight, nor a kind hello
'Cause the ears of humanity are closed to your call
And desensitized when you enter free fall

CLIFFHANGER

Hovering on the precipice of doubt and indecision
We hover, waiting, waiting, for the moment of precision

The 'maybes' and the 'what ifs' run rampant in our minds
Leaving threads of light and hope, trailing miserably behind

We listen to the mutterings replicated day by day
The promises of deeds to come, which slowly drift away

We ponder on the undertones, innuendo and assertions
Questioning the motives that provoke the dissertations

Frustrations and despair abound amidst the hollow soundings
Re-echoing across the land with vehemence astounding

The bumptious propagators of such unrelenting dogma
Provoke diverse reactions from the bearers of the stigma

Of fear and apprehension, despair and desperation
Of families diminishing and exiting our nation

Is there hope on the horizon, is there light beyond the clouds?
When the sun comes up tomorrow, will the life within applaud?

Let the truth shout from the rooftops; let the honesty shine through
For the future bears the hallmark of what's coming through for you

Sinking

Locked doors
Chained hearts
Where's the key?

Reins held
Tightly guarding
No entry zone

Super power
Hold control
Lest we weaken

Closed minds
Not for changing
There's the rub

Reached a crossroads
Where to now?
Neither left nor right

Need to listen
To the whisper
Where the answer's found

Unlock the doors
Unchain the hearts
Let go the reins

No need for guarding
Release control
We are not the power
Open minds
Times are changing

WHY?

Why do we do it? This self abuse
Destruct; refuse to see how much we hurt ourselves
Each other and the world, for generations, still
Unknowing of one man's folly

Why don't we listen to the words of wisdom, warning?
Vision – rushing at us from all sides, scared
Unfeeling, blind, unheeding for mankind

Are we so deaf, so blind, so out of love with all save our own ego?
Or do we drift in endless chaos and confusion?
So out of touch with the true source of love and beauty

AND JESUS WEPT!

They stare at you across the room, wide, empty, questioning
The eyes of innocents in a world untouched by love
Not guilty of their fate, but a grim reminder
of man's inhumanity to man

And Jesus Wept!

They sit on a cold stone pavement, beggars in a world of greed
Exposed to the ice-cold winds and ice-cold hearts
Not guilty of their fate, but a grim reminder
of man's inhumanity to man

And Jesus Wept!

They live in fear, these people blessed with autumn years
Alone, unsafe, unsure of who is friend and what the future holds
Not guilty of their fate, but a grim reminder
of man's inhumanity to man

And Jesus Wept!

Incinerators full to overflowing surplus to our needs
when man plays God
Wrong race, wrong colour, wrong age, wrong belief, wrong reason
Not guilty of their fate, but a grim reminder
of man's inhumanity to man
I stare with eyes that do not see and sit on sidelines
where talk is cheep
I live my life cocooned by good men's deeds, untouched,
comfortable, at ease
Not guilty of their fate, but a grim reminder
of man's inhumanity to man

And Jesus Wept!

My Soul Cries

Unseen tears fall like torrents and lodge in some hidden
expanse of space
That's what happens when my soul cries

Cavern's of pain and sadness surface like a volcanic eruption
That's what happens when my soul cries

Nobody sees what flows over the edge and across endless plains
That's what happens when my soul cries

It cannot be contained until it runs its circuitous course
That's what happens when my soul cries

It exposes with painful clarity what one thought long-forgotten
That's what happens when my soul cries

The resurrected debris of painful memories confront
my helpless spirit
That's what happens when my soul cries

My God where were you then
When my soul cried?

Where are you now
When my soul cries?
With your healing presence
While my soul cries

GETHSEMANE

My journey on to Calvary has long since begun
I'm overcome with sadness, I'm weighed down by your sin
Do not fall asleep on me; open up your eyes
I need you here to share my cross, don't you realise?

Chorus
Gethsemane, Gethsemane, a garden full of pain
Where Jesus sweated blood for us to cleanse us of our shame
You would not stay awake with me, in my time of trial
You would not watch one hour with me, one act of self-denial

I've lived with your rejection; your insults cause me pain
Your words have pierced my very soul, you still defile my name
You beat me and you stripped me, you nailed me to a tree
A crown of thorns now pierce my head, is this how you love me?

Chorus
Oh Lord, you have embraced your pain out of love for me
You suffered and you died for me so I would be free
What crosses you may send my way, is not for me to choose
Help me to embrace them all out of love for you

A Love Like I've Never Known

You'll have to love me a lot if I'm going to get through this pain
You are going to have to love me as you have never done before

You cannot know what is happening inside of me
and I hope you never will
You do not know the hurt that cuts deep and sharp
and leaves lifelong scars

How can you know the feelings that haunt my every
waking hour and from which there is no escape?
If I could show you my heart, you would see the damage,
and wonder how I still live?

What of the future?
Where is hope?
Where is mercy?

I've just seen it trickle away. And the past comes back
to remind me
That's why I need you to love me like never before,
if I am to face this world again

Present Moments

Do you hear the angels whisper, oh so gently in your ear?
Do you feel the spirit stirring when you know that they are near?
When you hear the church bells ringing,
does it fill your heart with joy?
Calm your throbbing spirit and peace to it apply
Have you heard the sound of birdsong as it ushers in the dawn?
Or seen the sun at daybreak as it lights up a new morn?
Have you seen the lightening strike the sky
and heard the claps of thunder?
And heard the sound of music and the rhythm of a drummer?
Does the lapping of the waves at sea soothe your weary; stressful mind?
And bear you to a higher place without an earthly bind?
Have you ever brushed a feather across your face or skin?
And felt the softness of the touch and the tremble deep within?
Have you tasted of the bitterness, the sorrow and the joy?
And felt the hearts responses as it struggled to reply
You have heard the children's laughter and the little baby's cry
The sound that stirs the heartstrings and can never be denied
Have you ever heard your heartbeat or felt your pulses race?
And wondered on the life in us by such amazing grace?
Can you smell a peat fire burning or the perfume of a rose?
Then draw it deep inside you so it never ever goes
And when the close of day comes and the sun sets in the sky
Have you watched that golden spectacle descending from on high?
Living in the present moment is a gift we cannot measure
As we gather all those cherished thoughts and memories
like a treasure

SPIRARE – SPIRIT BREATH

Deep calling to deep, silent wordless uttering's
Spirit to spirit, reflecting mutual longings of the heart
Stirred and moved into action or inactions
by a knowing beyond words
The still magnetism that draws rather than sets apart

Heart to heart, quiet confidences that welcome trust
Inviting into a cocooned space,
creating a web of intimate intrigue
Unwelcome intrusions, unsought and discouraged
Allowing gentle probing to filter through the layers of fatigue

Spirit to spirit, connecting at a level beyond understanding
Uplifting, energising, raising up a human spirit
To an awareness surpassing worldly comprehending
Gently arriving at a place of meaningful peace

You Are Just Something Mr. Cohen!

You are just something Mr. Cohen!
With your long, lean body, your husky voice
You hypnotize, you immobilise my thoughts
You come into my room and live my dream
Your droll, deep voice enthrals me
And seeps into my very being
It carries me away to dreamy places
The poetic charm of your words embraces
You are just something, Mr. Cohen!

Give me more days and nights like these
Keep me company with your languid eyes
Roll out the music and the background vocals
The continental rhythm of instrumental solos
The fedora becomes you, you wear it with style
Your warmth and your brilliance, stand out a mile
You are just something Mr. Cohen!

Wish I was there when you ran on stage
Looking so dapper, no way like your age
Wish I was there for your magic performance
Your lyrics of comfort, of prayer and of romance
You held everyone in the palm of your hand
The sheer captivation they couldn't understand
Hallelujah! You are just something Mr. Cohen!

A Different Drum

I heard the beat of a different drum
Thumping through the channels of my mind
The persistent call of a far off drummer
Channelling pathways of a different kind

It re-echoed down the years of my life
Amidst the rumblings of turbulence and strife
I journeyed with that messenger of sound
Moving against the tidal wave of a cultural mound

If sounds were words, what would I have heard?
If words were a call, would I have understood?

Amidst the density of noise or the deafening silence
Something takes hold of my heart and never relents
It clings like a leech and never stops beating
My constant companion, so I'm not competing
Yesterday or today, I could never resist it
Embracing, inspiring, outreaching, consistent

GIVE

Give joy to those whose hearts are sad
Give peace to those at war
Give tears to those with eyes of lead
To glisten like the stars

Give sight to those who cannot sea
And comfort those who mourn
Give of ourselves to those in need
That they may not be alone

Give our hands to those who falter
Those who cannot keep the pace
Let our homes be open shelter
To each colour, creed and race

Give time to those who need a friend
When everything looks bleak
And consolation too, extend
To all who comfort seek

Give love to all our children
From babyhood to teens
And share it out among them
Let hate never come between

Just Be There

I've been thinking just today
Of the times along the way
When we find life that much more than we can bear
But it's easier by far
When one's feeling below par
To know there's someone who will just be there

Be a face across the table, or an ear against the phone
Be that smile that brings a light into my life
Be that hand that reaches out when I'm low and all alone
Be whatever you must be, but just be there

Chorus
Just be there in the moments when my world has come apart
And it seems that life will never be the same
Something happens to my heart
And I get a real kick-start
When I know that as you've promised, you'll be there

Keep a candle in your window and a light within your heart
One that brings the glow of welcome to your eyes
There is nothing else on earth that will ease the pain and hurt
Then the knowing that you'll try to just be there

Chorus (X2)

Speak To My Heart

Speak gently to my heart
The words that chart
The course of my life's journey

Speak gently to my soul
Of the leading role
Your love plays in my life

Speak gently to my spirit
Of what I will inherit
When I've used the gifts you gave

Speak gently to my mind
In words so well defined
Your message of peace

Work gently through this channel
By word and example
To reflect your will

DYING EMBERS

Watching the flickering flames of the dying embers clash
Slowly letting go of light sparks as they turn to ash
Reflecting in the glowing stillness as memories come alive
And distant thoughts rise to the surface of a sleepy mind
Drifting through the haze of ponderous recollections
of forgotten days
Struggling to resurrect and pierce this fog where
deep buried relics laze

The sound of silence, hypnotic in the quiet of the fading hours
Taking on a distant hum as the spirit slowly disempowers
The mind willing these jumbled thoughts into non-existence
As it lurches tiredly towards rest and lulls itself
into a serene resistance

J'ESPERE!

I hope for a bright new morning with
The light of dawn on my face

I hope for a peace of heart within and
A sense of your amazing grace

J'espere!

I hope for the strength to take on board
Whatever the day may bring

I hope for a smile upon my face and
A song in my heart to sing

J'espere!

I hope that the clouds will part today
And reveal a heavenly blue

I hope that whatever the sun may shine
That it's warmth may rest on you

J'espere!

Skylight

Look up to the heavens, look up to the sky
Raise your vision upwards; hold your head up high
Look to right and left of you, look out all around
See beyond the barriers, where the light abounds
Look beyond the obvious, look way above the clouds
Peer above the parapet, way distant from the crowds

Why look down to earth below, when heaven is so near?
Why look for true happiness, when up here is no fear?

Look into the eyes of those you meet with every day
They tell a truer story, than words can ever say
Look into your heart today, where the love begins
Turn the key, undo the seals and reveal what lies within
Raise your vision skywards; raise your heart there too
Capture the light that's bursting through,
that's all you have to do